Chinese Modern New Technology Series

Online Shopping

Edited by Li Chaodong

Translated by Xuemeng Angela Li

河海大學出版社
HOHAI UNIVERSITY PRESS

ROYAL COLLINS
Books Beyond Boundaries

Dad, why do we come
to the bookshops?
Isn't it more convenient
to buy books online?
I bet you don't know about
this. Actually, online shopping
hasn't become a popular way
to buy things until recently.

Offline shopping has a significantly longer history than online shopping.

In ancient times, people lived a life of hunting and gathering. They exchange their spare items with others—the so-called "**barter exchange**."

Later, with the development of agriculture and farming, people start to process agricultural products. To facilitate the exchange process, people make arrangements to exchange items at a fixed location, which marks the earliest form of market. Some people even settle close to the market's location, leading to the formation of larger habitats.

Since the city's existence, the location and methods for exchange have become more regulated. In Western Zhou (1046–771 BC), the district market system was created to separate residential and commercial areas.

In the Chang'an City of the Tang Dynasty (AD 618–907), there were two large markets in the east and west where abundant products could be found. With spices, herbs, and jewelry from the West, tea and silk from the South, and leather goods from the North, products of exceptional quality all gathered in the two lively markets.

Diverse types of markets existed during the period. In addition to night and morning markets, special markets like temple fairs also appeared.

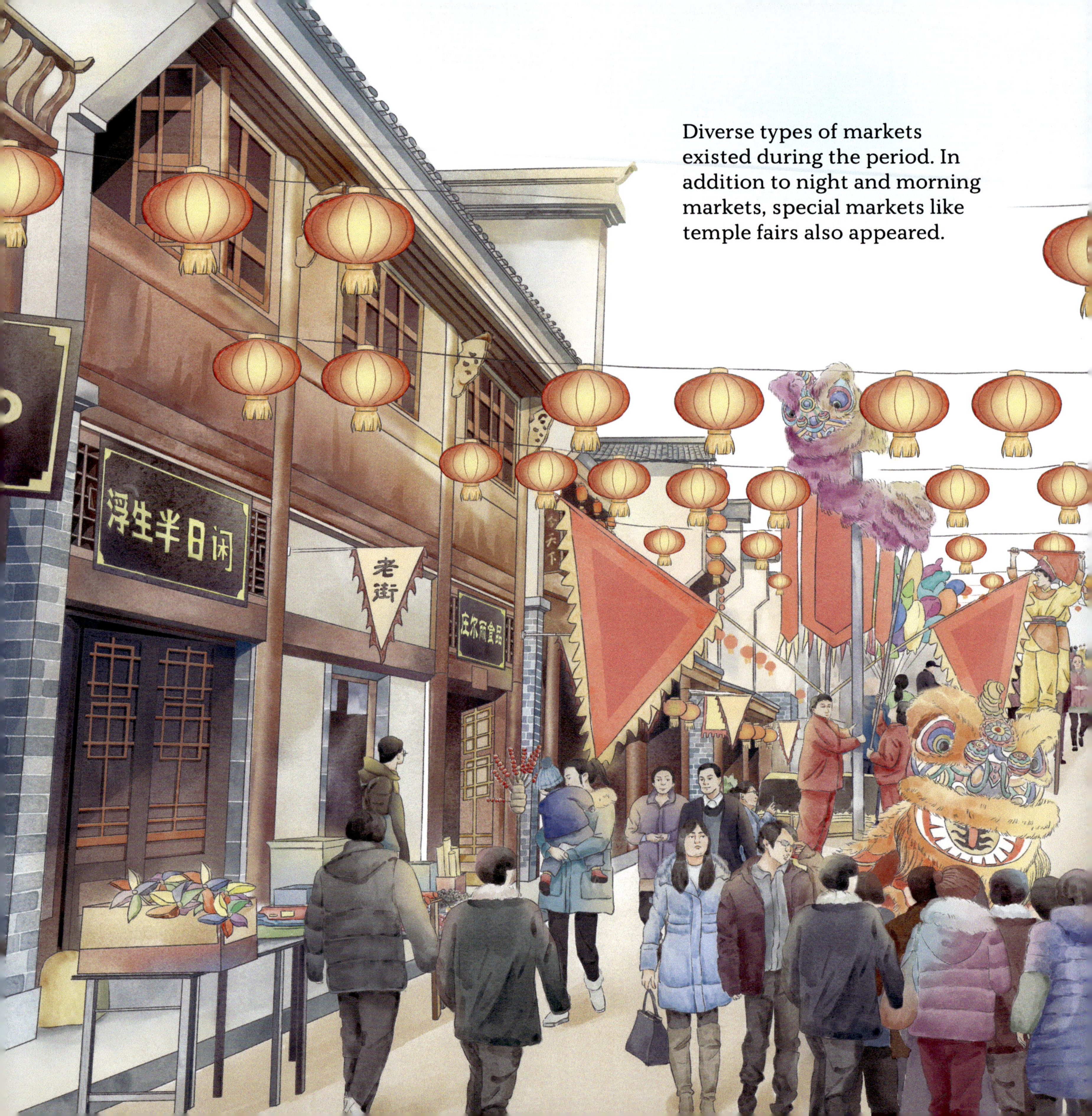

Temple fairs originated as a religious event to attract more followers.

It adds many entertaining activities to religious rituals in order to capture high participation.

Vendors set up all kinds of stalls outside around the temple, which gradually developed into a regular event.

"Home delivery" was also available during ancient times because of the inconvenience of transportation and limitations on the time and location of markets.

Therefore, some **street vendors** regularly carry goods and travel across the city to deliver to their customers.

These street vendors are also known as "the portable market." They picked goods that perfectly meet the daily needs of normal people, including toys, accessories, household goods, and tasty snacks.

After the Industrial Revolution, people began to mass-produce goods with machines in factories. The quantity and variety of products became increasingly high, creating a new location for exchange: **department stores**.

In the past, vendors and shops managed a limited variety of products, and people sometimes needed to visit many shops to purchase all the goods they needed. However, the department store gathered all categories of goods in one place, making it very convenient for customers.

Today's department stores are completely different from their early versions, where only household goods were sold. Nowadays, a lot more activities are available in department stores for people, such as eating and watching movies.

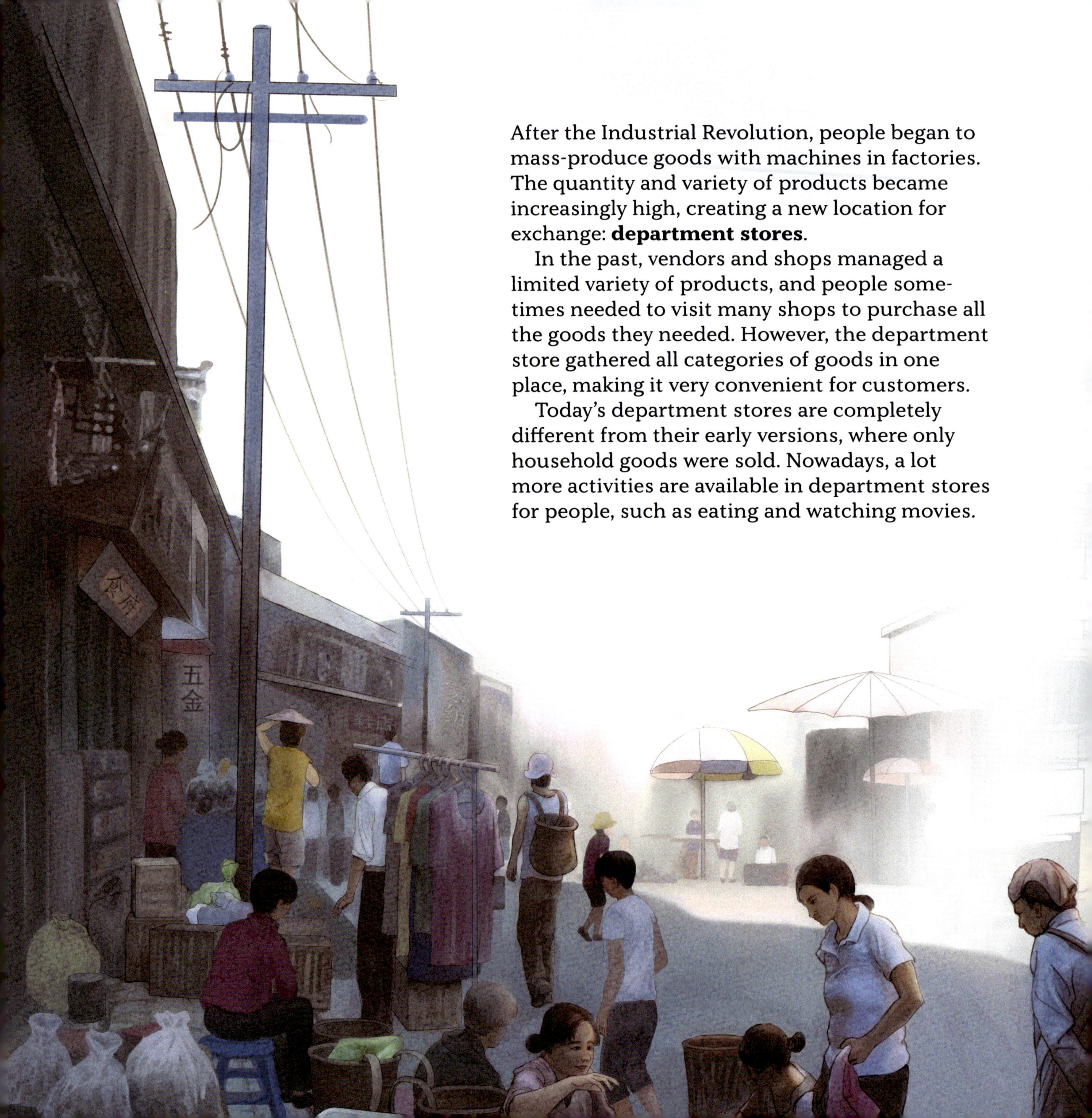

However, this has caused a new problem for department stores—price increases. Supermarkets thus appeared to meet people's demand for affordable shopping.

Vegetable and Fruits

After China joined the World Trade Organization (WTO), large franchise supermarkets thrived and made supermarket shelves the new place where people find their daily food and household goods.

Both the supermarkets and shopping malls struggled with limited capacity and high rent. Merchants need to pay high rent and bear tremendous costs to maintain their stores. The shopping experience is also unpleasant for some customers due to the wasted time and energy caused by the limited shopping space and long checkout lines.

In the 21st century, the rapid development of new technologies has made **online shopping** the new method for people's daily shopping for convenience.

Online shopping platforms act as a virtual large department store that gathers all the products from big shopping malls, small shops, supermarkets, restaurants, food markets, and bookstores, regardless of location.

The Four Pillars of Online Shopping

Computers are incredibly smart and can remember many numbers and calculate quickly. It never makes a mistake, even when billions of people purchase simultaneously on the same platform.

Convenient **payment methods** have also advanced the development of online shopping. The payment process of online shopping used to be very complicated. It requires us to first register for a U-key at the bank and then plug the key into the computer to pay. Now, online shopping supports payment through various payment platforms, which is convenient, fast, and safe. China's payment technology is currently in a leading position around the world.

The convenience of online shopping was also inseparable from the developed **logistics services** in China. The little package we received has actually gone through many steps, including packaging, storage, transportation, loading and unloading, and delivery. An automated sorting system was also built to facilitate the process of logistics and transportation, which deploys robots to help sort the parcels!

The popularization of smartphones allows everyone to complete their shopping within a few taps.

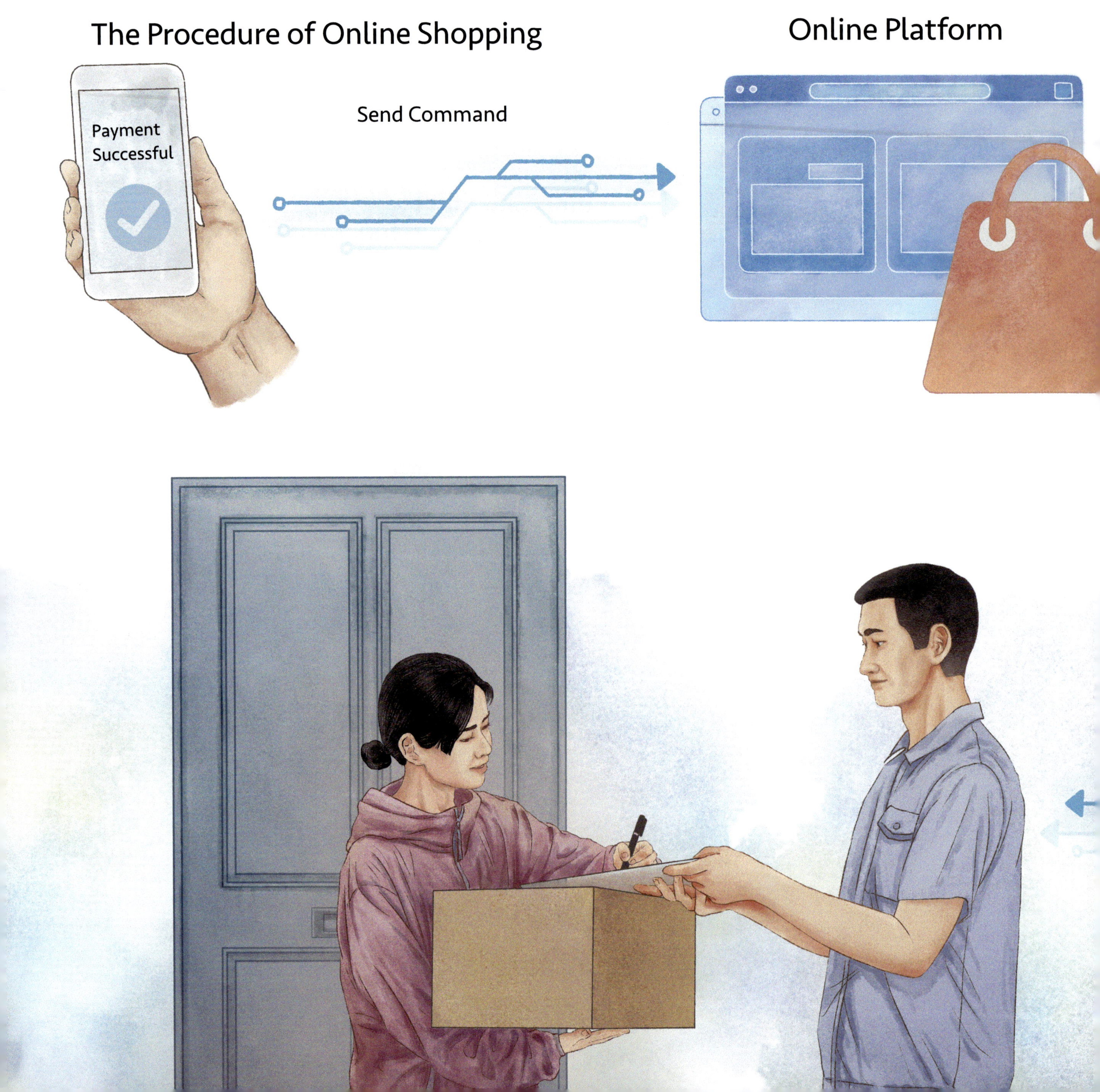
The Procedure of Online Shopping
Online Platform
Payment
Successful
Send Command

Order Notification

Online shopping is not limited by time and location and offers more options to consumers. Some products even come with lower prices than other channels.

Warehouse of Merchants

Packaging

Logistics and Transportation

The development of online shopping depends on new technologies. Its popularization brought convenience to certain people, but also created inconvenience to those who haven't learned about it.

In addition, offline shopping is more than a purchase. It offers an emotional experience to the customers as well. Online shopping, on the other hand, cannot offer people immersive experiences such as comfortable shopping spaces, art and cultural scenes, entertaining and leisure activities, and social interactions.

Because of that, the form of online shopping has been constantly upgrading. The previous major form of online shopping relied on users finding products on their own. Buyers who know what they want can search for goods through the shopping platform themselves and place an order to buy.

With the prevalence of the Internet, the maturity of algorithms, and the diversified development of consumer demands, online shopping has gradually transformed into the form of product recommendation. Merchants can attract consumers and encourage their purchases by advertising on the platforms.

Nowadays, online shopping can augment the interactive shopping experience through various technologies. By using specialized devices, we can try on different clothes and visit luxurious residencies thousands of miles away with an immersive view.

Online shopping has been constantly optimizing the immersive experience of customers and satisfying their diversified demands. By combining online and offline shopping, people can purchase products online first and then pick them up in offline member stores and enjoy in-store services. They can also select their preferred products in-store and order through the online platform. With online shopping extending into reality and offline stores bridging with virtual platforms, the two shopping experiences have become complementary and interdependent.

Traditional Sales Model

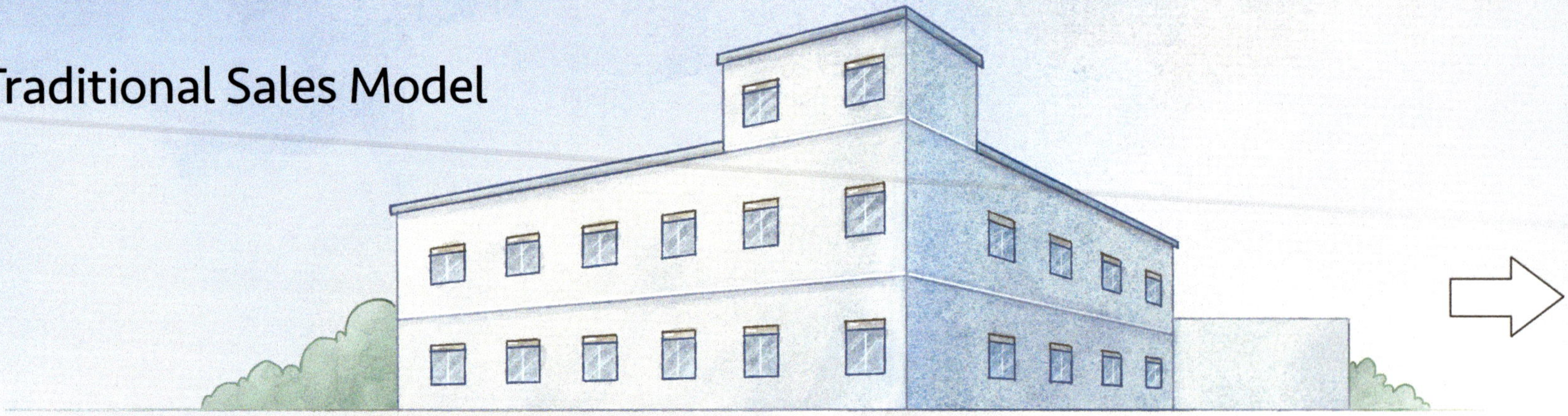

Online Sales Model

The rapid development of online shopping has broadened people's horizons. Traditional sales models have also been constantly upgrading. The seamless interface of customers, online platforms, and products at any time and location has become a reality.

The Internet of Things (IoT) has reformed the commercial sector tremendously. It reflects valuable data in real time and provides directions for market development.

Agents at All Levels (Offline Stores)
Customer
Customer
闲置出售
双十一
换购
退货
今日推荐
海淘

Online shopping has become an inseparable part of our daily lives.

The scale of online shoppers in China has exceeded 800 million.

The popularity of Chinese products even spread to foreign markets through e-commerce platforms, making the total transaction volume of the Chinese e-commerce industry far ahead of others.

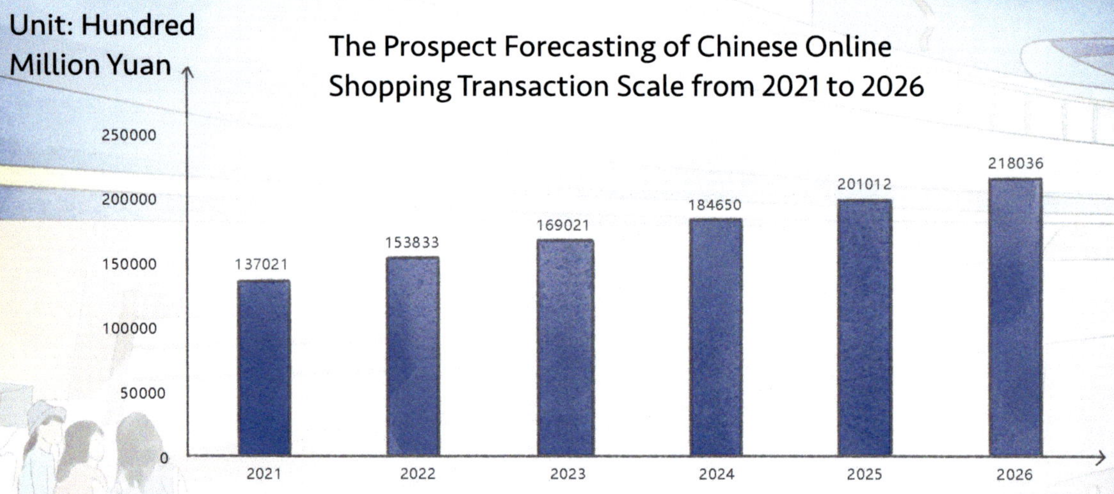

From barter exchange to online shopping, the development of the Chinese shopping style reflects people's aspirations for a beautiful life and their persistent pursuit. The development of online shopping is firmly backed by the diligent, brave, and resilient spirit of Chinese people.

Chinese Modern New Technology Series
Online Shopping

Edited by Li Chaodong
Translated by Xuemeng Angela Li

First published in 2024 by Royal Collins Publishing Group Inc.
Groupe Publication Royal Collins Inc.
550-555 boul. René-Lévesque O Montréal (Québec) H2Z1B1 Canada

ISBN: 978-1-4878-1238-6

To find out more about our publications, please visit www.royalcollins.com.